POOR HEALTH, RICH PROFITS

Multinational Drug Companies and the Third World

Poor Health, Rich Profits

Multinational Drug Companies and the Third World

by Tom Heller

SPOKESMAN BOOKS

First Published in 1977

Cloth ISBN 0 85124 168 9
Paper ISBN 0 85124 169 7

Published by the Bertrand Russell Peace Foundation Ltd., Bertrand Russell House, Gamble Street, Nottingham for

Spokesman Books

Printed by the Russell Press Ltd., Nottingham

Contents

Introduction

This book attempts to describe the present structure of the international pharmaceutical industry as it relates to the less developed countries.

It shows that the less developed countries are an important and rapidly expanding market for the large multinational drug companies. Although a great deal of profit is made from these activities in the third world, it appears that the companies give back little tangible in return. The majority of the companies' efforts are used to research and develop the medicines that are suited to the markets of the developed world, while scant regard is paid to the particular needs of the medical conditions predominant in the developing countries.

The medicines are sold in the third world using intensive advertising techniques which are subject to fewer controls than in the West, and open to unscrupulous practices. The medicines sold in this way are very expensive, and perfectly acceptable alternative medicines, which would be much cheaper, are not promoted.

It is frequently claimed that the presence of these large companies operating within the developing world actively assists "development" by a steady transfer of technology. This book examines this claim, and argues that the entire structure of multinational companies depends on the total control over such technology, and that there has been virtually *no* transfer of relevant technology by these companies to the countries of the developing world. By using the power that control over technology brings, the companies have in fact eliminated many potential competitors and prevented indigenous pharmaceutical industries developing to meet the real needs of the people of the third world.

The book goes on to examine the various ways in which governments of some enlightened third world countries have attempted to impose controls over the pharmaceutical industry as presently organized, and makes recommendations for action within the developed and developing countries.

This book is intended as a small contribution to a much larger debate concerning the structure, function and effects of the multinational companies in general. There is now a wealth of evidence to suggest that no real distinctions should be drawn between the functioning of these companies in the developed and underdeveloped nations, and that their striving for growth and gain is frequently at the expense of entire nations and the majority of their peoples in whatever country they operate.

There is further current debate about the role of pharmaceutical products in the promotion of health. The present emphasis on curative medicine throughout the world, and the patterns of delivery of health care are under close scrutiny. Pharmaceutical products for both preventive and curative purposes will presumably always be required, whatever the shape of the health services of the future, and the most effective way of developing, manufacturing and distributing these products is the concern of this book.

I

The Multinational Pharmaceutical Industry and the Third World

There is an increasing concern about the operations and controls exerted over the large multinational companies. They certainly are very large and powerful organisations, and their turnovers often are larger than the gross national products of small developing nations. Much of the attention centred on these organisations is dismissed by them as propaganda or paranoia. There is, however, sufficient empirical evidence about their activities to cause concern to all those interested in the effect that these large companies have throughout the world, and in particular in the developing nations. Hard evidence about the activities of these companies is notoriously difficult to obtain, and their refusal to cooperate in investigations, even when requested to do so by the governments of developed nations,[1] should lead us to question the position of the less developed nations who also need to exert effective controls over the activities of these companies operating on their territory.

The less developed countries are underdeveloped in many respects besides the purely economic aspects that have been the subject of so much attention. Thus their control procedures over the functioning of the multinational companies (MNCs), which could serve as a countermanding power against the obvious economic power of the companies, are also underdeveloped.[2] Their taxation laws are often cumbersome and antiquated, and officials in the taxation and customs departments might be of comparatively low educational standard. The domestic competition within the third world countries themselves will not have highly developed commercial training, particular technical skills, or access to sufficient credit facilities, and will probably be poor competitors against the incoming MNCs. The labour and consumer organisations in the host countries are usually comparatively unorganised, and can certainly exert little effective international power. Similarly, controls over such diverse functions as quality control, patent licensing and advertising standards are usually in an early stage of development.

None of the current literature exploring the relationship between the MNCs and the peoples of the third world suggests that all large companies are evil, and working consciously against the best interests of the third world. There is, however, increasing examination of the structure of these companies, and debate as to whether it is possible within the structure of these companies, to ensure that the real needs of the majority of the people within the developing nations can be met.

The massive pharmaceutical companies exist primarily to make money, not to produce and distribute the cheapest effective medicine to the most people in need. What evidence is there that these two ends are incompatible? Could the present system be adjusted and controlled sufficiently in order that the bulk of the world's population no longer has to go without medicines or any sort?

Concern over these issues is not the exclusive domain of militant organisations, but is shared by many international organisations including several of the branches of the United Nations (UNCTAD, ECOSOC, UNIDO, UNRISD)[3], the International Labour Organisation, the International Confederation of Free Trade Unions, as well as a great many governments of developed and developing nations.[4]

The general nature of the relationship between multinational companies and the less developed countries

In the less developed countries (LDCs) there is generally a very limited history of indigenous scientific, technical or manufacturing effort and often virtually no infrastructure of supportive, integrating industries. Therefore if these countries want the products of advanced technology, they have to bargain for them from the developed world. The governments of the LDCs are naturally loth to continually buy such goods in a finished form with their scarce foreign reserves, and are keen to arrange for their production in their own country utilising some local finance and the local labour force.

The initial entry of the multinational companies appears very attractive to the decision-making élite within the developing countries. They are often in need of foreign exchange, and it is hoped that the establishment of subsidiaries of multinational companies on their soil will enable them to learn the necessary technology to enable them to produce the goods for themselves in the future. At the time of the first involvement of these companies the benefits accrue only to a very small minority (viz the same decision-making élite who can afford their products, and the small number of employees), it is hoped that in time benefits will "trickle down" to the remainder of the population. There is now considerable evidence to show that this does not happen. Even with a rapidly rising Gross National Product, the standard of living of the poorest sections of the community fails to improve and the gap between rich and poor within the country grows ever larger.[9] Indeed it is even claimed by some economists that the involvement of multinational concerns is one of the primary factors *causing* underdevelopment through their effect on income distribution, the elimination of indigenous industry and the failure to transfer the appropriate technology.[69]

The major source of power of these MNCs is in their control over the technology necessary to produce and market these advanced products, and they can hardly be expected to give away their know-how free to the less developed nations, who might become competitors. For this reason the MNCs require patent protection for their products and processes and often for the machinery used to produce them. They claim that use of patents for this protection, which gives a certain number of years free from competition, allows them to make the profit which is essential to stimulate and finance further discovery and development of new products. They are prepared to establish production and marketing facilities only when provided with adequate patent protection, and claim that the facilities established, as well as the inflow of foreign capital and expertise, will actively assist the transfer of relevant technological skills to the host country.

The exact role of the patents in the developing nations is, however, not quite as simple as this.[5] Possibly some of these arguments might be valid for Western markets, but there is growing evidence that the actual use of patents leads to restrictive practices, the establishment of monopoly market positions and a *reduction* in foreign investment in manufacturing, leading to adverse terms of trade and deficits in the balance of payments of the host countries.[6] The majority of patents holdings in the developing world are owned by foreign interests, and there is evidence that those held by the nationals are of little economic or industrial importance.

Table 1[6]

Patents granted to foreigners as a percentage of total patents granted between 1957 and 1961 inclusive.

Country	*Percentage*
India	89.4
Turkey	91.7
United Arab Republic	93.0
Trinidad and Tobago	94.2
Pakistan	95.8

A majority of the patents taken out by foreign interests are neither used, nor given as licences for use by others. The granting of patents licences is often tied by the foreign companies to conditions for their use, which include export restrictions on the goods manufactured, and tied purchase of other goods from the granting company. It is hard to avoid the fact that the use of patents in this way is detrimental to the best interests of the third world.

The monopoly positions held by foreign firms mean that the indigenous industry is unlikely to be able to develop really competitive products. The technology owned and controlled by foreign interests, and protected by the patent laws, will be superior to local industry, and will lead surely to the establishment of a two-tier system, with the multinationals producing all the modern, high-technology, high-profit goods, with indigenous industry far behind in non-competitive, old-fashioned products. Imported industry also competes with the local firms in attempting to capture local finance. The MNCs are at a great advantage in this venture because they have the vast capital resources of the parent company to back them, and are often close associates of the multinational credit banks. When coupled with superior, imported skills in advertising and management it is small wonder that local firms are at a disadvantage, and are frequently taken over completely by incoming MNCs thereby further enhancing foreign monopoly positions.

This build-up of high-technology, capital-intensive, labour-saving industry, developed for Western economies, is not necessarily well suited to the host country. Often it is introduced into countries faced with high levels of unemployment and very little capital, especially foreign exchange, to invest. A study of all modern manufacturing industry of this type in Latin America showed that, while it increased its share of the national product from 11.0 per cent in 1925 to 25 per cent in 1970, the proportion of the workforce employed fell from 14.4 per cent to 13.8 per cent[7] It seems clear that these firms *eliminate* more jobs than they create by the use of inappropriate technology. Certainly in the multinational pharmaceutical industry it has been shown that labour accounts for only 3.4 per cent of total costs.[8]

The sale of technology is one of the most difficult areas to assess, but estimation of the value of technology transferred is vital to the financial management of these companies. The parent company is in a position to sell its technology to its subsidiary in a less developed country, and the cost it puts on this, both as an initial fixed investment, and as continuing royalty and fee payments for managerial and technical assistance, will be vital to the amount of profit that it can be said to have made from the subsidiary. Thus the parent company will wish to keep the declared value of the transferred technology high in order to maximise its apparent contribution to the subsidiary's finance. However, when detailed investigation of the actual value of this transferred technology has been made, gross over-estimates of its value have been placed on this technology by the parent companies.[10]

Similarly, many anomalies have been found to exist when the parent companies have put prices on intermediate products sold to their subsidiaries in developing countries.[11] The greater value that can be attributed to these "transfer prices," the greater return can be made by the parent without being subject to accusations of making excess profit. The fullest studies on anomalies in transfer prices in excess of "arm's length" prices, available on the world market, have come from several industries in Columbia.[12]

Thus the reported profits in subsidiary companies need bear little relation to actuality. The same study quoted above[12] showed that the *reported* average rate of return from the Columbian drug industry between 1960 and 1968 was only 6.4 per cent. A conservative estimate accounting for anomalies in transfer pricing and royalty payments brought the *actual* figure to 137 per cent[10]

The use of tax-havens is common practice, and passing products through Panama, the Bahamas or Lichtenstein when importing or exporting, can lead to great flexibility in the level of taxation paid in either host or parent country.

The MNCs are keen to use local finance whenever possible in establishing subsidiaries. The contribution from the parent is often not in the form of money, but as technology or equipment. Some studies have evaluated the respective contributions of investment in subsidiary companies. For the years 1957-1965 analysis was made of the entire investment pattern in South American subsidiaries of MNCs. Only 17 per cent of the gross investment was found to come from the parent country, while the remaining 83 per cent was financed from sources within the host country, either from local savings or re-invested earnings of the subsidiary. Over the period 1960-1968 the same MNCs repatriated 79 per cent of the net profits, however, not to mention the additional remissions of royalties, interest and other fees.[13]

II

The Role of the Multinational Pharmaceutical Concerns

In the next chapters we shall go on to examine the multinational pharmaceutical industry, to see if the general observations can be shown to hold specifically for this socially important industry. Schifrin has said: "The identification of these flaws and problems is not, of course, the objective of critics. The essential goal they are pursuing is the area of social policy: bringing about changes in the web of rules and conditions that determine the behaviour of drug companies, so as to create stronger and more compelling pressures for more socially efficient patterns of resource use and product pricing."[14]

It is important at this stage to examine how the drug companies see themselves. Some clue can be obtained from a speech made by John J. Powers, Jr., the Hon. Chairman of the board of Pfizer, the world's eighth largest drug company. In reply to the report of the UN "group of 20 eminent persons"[53] set up to examine the role of multinational companies, he said:

> "It is important not to overdramatise the role of the multinational companies and attribute to them tensions and problems within domestic societies and in international relations which arise, not from the MNCs themselves, but from the basic forces of change now ranging throughout the world. There is nothing mysterious or sinister about MNCs, nor grand and heroic. It endangers the discussion to

view them in such terms. *They are an effect, not the cause,* of global forces which far transcend them. They are a response to a world economy."[15]

Let us for the moment accept this passive picture of multinational companies, and deny the critics who argue about the intrinsic dynamics that exist within a large company, both in economic and personal terms, striving for ever-increasing expansion, and who produce evidence that this expansion is frequently to the detriment of the countries in which they have their operations.[68] If the multinational companies are simply the response to social, political and economic factors, and not a cause of them, they will continue to operate up to the limits imposed upon them by the laws of the countries in which they operate. It is not relevant to this argument that there are proven cases where this passive picture has been shown not to apply (e.g. the involvement of ITT in Chile) and where large firms have thought it their concern to enter into the business of attempting to influence social and political systems. The generally passive picture of the role of MNCs would suggest that where there are poor, under-developed restraint procedures, some companies will use the situation to maximise returns. This has certainly been shown by many cases involving the activities of these companies in "developed" Western countries (e.g. Ferranti, Roche, etc. in the UK, and the myriad of cases exposed in the USA). In the "underdeveloped" countries, where control procedures are even less sophisticated, and in the apparent absence of any internal restraining procedures, a proportion of the drug companies will utilise the inequalities of control standards, to the obvious detriment of the peoples of the third world. It is for this reason that we should work to produce uniform systems of control and monitoring which can be internationally developed and internationally enforced, affording equal protection for all.

The role of the pharmaceutical companies should also be examined in the context of their effect on health care delivery systems in the countries in which they market their products. It is now generally accepted that the bulk of disease in the underdeveloped countries is the effect of poor socio-economic conditions (poor housing, nutrition etc.). Certainly the improvements in the morbidity and mortality patterns that have occurred in the West have largely been the result of improvements in these standards.[16] The contribution to the health of people in the third world made by a health service that is organised towards curative medicine would appear to be very small indeed. It is to the advantage of the drug companies, however, that the health services remain orientated towards a curative approach, and they divert virtually their entire advertising effort to the promotion of products used for curative medicine. Thus the pressure of the drug companies is exerted in such a way as to maintain the present emphasis on curative medicine and to maximise the proportion of the health budget that is spent on pharmaceutical products.

The entire structure and organisation of the drug companies at present depends on the production of "new and improved" medicines. The vast majority of these "new" products do not represent any significant therapeutic advance, but are the result of molecular juggling to produce a product just sufficiently

Table 2[71]

Percentage of current expenditure on personal health services spent on medicaments.

Country	*Year*	*Percentage spent on medicaments*
United Kingdom	1961/2	8.7
Philippines	1961/2	29.6
Venezuela	1962	26.4

different to satisfy the requirements for granting a new period of patent protection. These "me-too" drugs are tailor-made for the *market* requirements of the developed world. In fact the medicines required for almost the entire range of use in the third world are covered by a fairly small list of cheap, yet effective products, often no longer covered by patent protection. Segall has made a list of "first-line" pharmaceuticals that would cover the general pattern of needs in a typical underdeveloped country.[70] This list is reproduced at the end of this book as an Appendix.

It should be noted that we do not advocate that second-best medicines are good enough for use in the third world, or that the people of the developing nations should be denied access to the full effective therapeutic range. The products of real therapeutic advances should be made available throughout the world, but where there exist cheaper, appropriate alternatives to the products of the MNCs, these should certainly be considered for use in the third world.

III

The Structure of the Industry

The pharmaceutical industry is one of the most mulinational of all industries with a total world market (excluding the centrally planned economies) of £7,100 m. The industry is dominated by a number of super-sized corporations.

These top companies probably account for about 60 per cent of total world sales, and more than 90 per cent of total research and development effort.

Although any one of these firms might have only a 5-10 per cent share of the total world market, the market is fragmented into sub-specialties and a single firm could have a virtual monopoly in its specialised field (e.g., Roche holds about 70 per cent of the UK market in tranquillisers, and in the USA in each of the 13 major therapeutic groups the four leading firms accounted for 60-80 per cent or more of the sales).

The industry spends more than any other manufacturing industry on research and development, currently between 7-12 per cent of total sales.[1] This research is extremely expensive and increasingly the preserve of the very largest firms. The cost of discovering and marketing a new drug has been quoted by Dr Spinks, research director of ICI, as leaping from £1m in 1952 to £5m in 1972.[19] It is small wonder that these

Table 3[18]

The world pharmaceutical industry

Company	*Nationality*	*1970 turnover in pharmaceuticals ($millions)*
1. Roche	Switzerland	840
2. Merck	USA	670
3. Hoeschst	W. Germany	497
4. Ciba-Geigy	Switzerland	492
5. American Home Products	USA	479
6. Lilly	USA	421
7. Sterling	USA	418
8. Pfizer	USA	416
9. Warner-Lambert	USA	408
10. Sandoz	Switzerland	346
11. Upjohn	USA	342
12. Abbott	USA	330
13. ER Squibb	USA	310
14. Bayer	W Germany	286
15. Bristol-Myers	USA	262
16. Glaxo	UK	261
17. Rhone-Poulenc	France	257
18. Scherin-Plough	USA	255
19. Cyanamid	USA	243
20. Smith Kline & French	USA	215
21. Boehringer-Ingleheim	W Germany	211
22. Schering AG	W Germany	211
23. Takeda	Japan	209
24. Roussel-UCLAF	France	183
25. Wellcome	UK	136
26. Beecham	UK	132
27. Searle	USA	125
28. Azko	Holland	121

firms will only undertake research at all if they will be able to recoup this cost from profits. This research effort has to be directed towards those products with the largest market. This is clearly shown by the figures published by the Pharmaceutical Manufacturers' Association Annual Survey (1973):[20]

Table 4[20]

Category of drug	*Percentage share of domestic market*	*Percentage share of applied research and development*
CNS	25.7	17.4
Anti-infectives	16.0	15.8
Neoplasms	11.8	15.4
Cardiovascular	8.7	12.8
Digestive	11.2	6.0
Diagnostic	4.4	5.1
Dermatologicals	3.1	4.1
Biologicals	2.7	4.0
Respiratory	6.0	3.9
Vitamins	7.8	2.0

The pressure to recoup money for continuing research and development (R &D) costs, and to make a profit from their operations, leads to a continuous striving to discover, develop and market new products. The competition between medicines is usually in terms of "product" rather than "price" and doctors are encouraged to prescribe the named manufacturer's brand of product, often without comparing its price with potential rivals. Thus the industry sells its products using brand names rather than the name of the active ingredients (generic name) which might be marketed by several firms. The selling of medicines is in itself a necessary part of the industry and is done largely by the promotion of brand names by representatives of the drug firms (detail men) and by advertisments in the medical literature. The promotion and sales costs are much greater than the average for manufacturing industry and again small firms find it hard to mount the size of campaign necessary to enter competition against the massive multinationals.

Table 5[21 and 1]

Advertising volume as percentage of sales by product category, 1972

	Percentage
UK Pharmaceuticals	14.6
USA Drugs & cosmetics	10.9
Food	4.0
Cars	0.7
Soft drinks	6.4
Tyres	1.8
Total average all industry USA	1.9

Controls over the introduction and marketing of new products are enforced by countries separately and there is as yet no international set of standards to monitor these functions. Thus the rigours of the toxicity testing and proof of efficiency of new drugs varies from country to country. In America the Federal Drugs Administration (FDA) laws are probably the most stringent in the world, and testing for toxicity may take several years and be the largest portion of the research expenditure. The documents recently submitted to the FDA requesting permission to introduce a new anti-Parkinsonism drug consisted of 504 documents, each 4.8 cms thick. The total height of the finished dossier was 24 metres![22] Spinks estimates that the cost of this toxicity testing represents about £4m of the £5m research cost for each new product.[19]

New products and processes are patented by the firms to prevent others utilising the fruits of their research efforts. At present there is no uniformity for granting patents and while some countries have stringent patent laws, others offer no protection at all (e.g. Brazil, Italy and South Korea).

All these factors tend to make the large, successful firms even larger and more successful and enhance their monopoly positions. Small companies just cannot afford the vast sums of money needed for research development, toxicity testing, patent protection and marketing. The large companies themselves cannot risk these massive amounts on products that will not be commercially successful. The NEDO estimate is that only products likely to achieve annual sales of at least £4-£5m will be worth doing any major research to discover.[17]

Even with such large outlays and with such apparent risk involved in their operations, the pharmaceutical industry is one of the most profitable of all manufacturing industries.

Table 6[21 and 1]

		Profit rate percentage
United Kingdom (1969)	All manufacturing industry	12.6
	Boots	19.2
	Glaxo	26.3
	Beecham	28.4
United States (1972)	All US manufacturers	10.6
	All US drug manufacturers	13.8

The amount of information released by the industry is not sufficiently detailed to make an objective analysis. Using the same statistics, two widely divergent views have emerged – one camp supporting the present structure of the industry and the other wanting radical change. Rather than enter further into this debate we shall present a simplified outline of the arguments put forward by each side.[23] We shall confine our opinions to the later sections of this report, examining how the structure of the pharmaceutical industry in the West affects those living in the Third World.

The industry	**The critics**
1. *Size:* The larger the firm the more likely it is to make significant contributions to advances in medical science by increasing the size of its research effort. There will be less wastage and duplication of marketing and administrative effort leading ultimately to cheaper, better medicines.	The larger the firm the greater its monopoly position and the smaller the chance for competition. This competition would increase the rate of new products and lower the price of medicines through price competition. Larger budgets for research don't necessarily improve the rate of innovation and there is no evidence so far that increasing the size of firms has brought any prices down.
2. *Research and Development* The sums of money now spent on R & D mean that the end result must be a drug that will be commercially viable and can also finance the R & D of the future.	The majority of R & D is spent on "me-too" drugs using molecular manipulation designed to produce a product which is profitable but not necessarily an advance for science. The necessary commercial end for all R & D effort damages innovatative activity.

3. *Risk and profit:*

Many lines of research terminate in expensive dead ends. Therefore when a drug is commercially successful it has to pay for itself and for its non-viable counterparts. "I have yet to hear of a fund being set up for the relief of distressed pharmaceutical firms which conscientiously attempted to carry out research on the rarer diseases in the hope of finding a remedy, and went bankrupt."[24]

The element of risk is grossly overstated, and used as a means of increasing profits. In fact no large firms recently have been unsuccessful in making large profits and positions in sales and profit league tables remain remarkably static, which would be the opposite if real risk were involved. The top 20 list of companies has contained only 21 names over the last seven years.[14]

4. *Patents:*

The use of patents protects the firm from competition for some time. Thus drugs can be guaranteed a market and will be able to make profits for the company. The use of strong patent protection will lead to an *increased* rate of innovation as firms naturally want to discover and market new profitable drugs.

Governments should not have the power to break patents by granting compulsory licences.

The use of patents protects the monopoly position of firms. They are thus able to make excessive profits from their products freed from price competition. Patent protection *blocks* competitive initiative from other firms.

Governments should be able to grant compulsory licenses if it is in the best interests of the general public that competition should take place.

5. *Generic names:*

The use of brand names is advisable so that doctors can be assured of the quality of the product. The manufacture of medicines by reputable firms and marketing under brand names ensures a high quality and high level

The prescribing by use of brand names enhances the monopoly position of large firms and ensures the maintenance of high prices and excessive profit.

The brand names obscure the pharmacological properties of the compound, which of accountability. Generic products might be cheaper simply because rigorous quality controls have been skimped.

is contained in the generic name. If the doctor is keen that the medicine should be made by a particular firm, he should name the firm next to the generic name of the drug.

6. *Toxicity testing and product information:*

There is already sufficient bureaucratic constraint on the drug firms. This is time-consuming and expensive and will lead to a slower rate of innovation or increased cost for the consumer.

There should be internationally acceptable regulations concerning drug testing and information. This will protect the consumer and uniformity will lead to speedier introduction of new products. Local variations would be acceptable if a valid reason is given.

7. *Profits:*

The profits that are made are essential to make enough money to promote further R & D.

Release of detailed information about the companies' financial transactions would give advantage to competitors. Voluntary Price Regulation is sufficient, coupled with normal competitive forces within the industry to keep prices at the optimal level for everybody. Government interference is definitely not necessary.

The profits made by some firms are excessive and will lead to increased cost to the patient, either directly or through Government health services expenditure. More information is needed so that there can be control over excess profits.

Voluntary price schemes don't always work, and some firms don't cooperate. Tight government control is essential.

8. *Advertising and marketing:*
Intensive advertising effort is needed to sell the medicines and to inform the doctors of the new, improved products. The more medicine that is sold, the cheaper it will be

A vast amount of money is spent on advertising the medicines which could be better spent on research or in making the medicines cheaper. The advertising is often not really informative, especially for the patients. The drug representatives do a very useful job informing the medical profession. The use of the latest advertising techniques is justifiable if it sells more of the product. Voluntary control is sufficient over advertising standards.

regarding comparative prices. Most of the effort is put into promoting brand names and the information content is low.

Gimmicks are not appropriate to the sale of medicines. Tight government control is essential over advertising standards.

IV

How the Multinationals Operate

The underdeveloped countries represent a very important part of the world market in pharmaceuticals, taking almost 30 per cent of total imports of world production.

Table 7[66]

International trade in medicinal products, 1971 ($millions)

	Exports	*Imports*	*Balance*	*Percentage of total Exports*	*Imports*
Developed Market-economy countries	2,757	1,833	924	81.1	56.5
Southern European countries	36	182	146	1.1	5.6
Developing countries	231	905	674	6.8	27.9
Socialist countries of Eastern Europe	375	327	48	11.0	10.1
Total	3,399	3,247	152	100.0	100.1

The breakdown of the destination of US pharmaceutical exports shows how important sales to the developing countries are to the export perfomance of the industry.

Table 8[20]

Destination of US Pharmaceutical exports, 1968

(Percentages)

Canada	8.8
Europe	31.3
Latin America	23.7
Asia	19.2
Near East	6.0
Africa	4.7
Other	6.3

Projections for the future indicate that a substantial portion of the growth of the industry will probably take place through sales in the Third World.

Table 9[17]

World market for human medicines: Projection of demand, 1969-1980

	Total World Market ($m)		*Third World Market ($m)*	
1969	14,363		3,514	
	Upper projection	lower projection	upper projection	lower projection
1980	48,680	37,399	11,522	8,533

The sale of pharmaceuticals abroad is highly profitable for the companies concerned. The Beecham group in 1970 made 71 per cent of its profits from sales abroad, and profit margins on overseas sales were twice as high as on home sales.

Within the less developed countries themselves, the multinational companies often have a majority share of the market.

The structure of the indigenous industry that the multinational companies meet as competitors within

Table 10[26, 27, 28]

Country	Year	Share of market (percentages) Local	Multinational company
Brazil	1969	22	78
Argentina	1969	35	65
Peru	1964	5	95
Philippines	1966	20	80
India	1969	25-35	65-75
Venezuela	1970	10	90

developing countries is very variable, and depends on the degree of industrial development that has taken place in the country concerned. The United Nations Industrial Development Organisation has divided the stages of development needed to produce pharmaceutical products into five, ranging from 'no pharmaceutical manufacturing' to 'the presence of established industry'. Not surprisingly, the majority of Third World countries come within the first two stages, and none at all are classified in the fifth stage.

Transfer of technology to the less developed countries

As has been mentioned earlier, the major source of the power of the multinational companies lies in their control over the technology required to produce and market their products. It has also been argued that in the case of the pharmaceutical industry at least, this highly advanced technology is not always the most appropriate for use in developing countries. It is frequently claimed by the companies themselves, however, that the presence of their subsidiaries within the developed world helps in the transfer of necessary technology. We shall now examine that claim.

Technology involved in basic research and development.

At this time virtually no basic research and development is done by the MNCs within the Third World itself, thus virtually precluding the transfer of this essential, basic technology. We have already demonstrated in Table 4 that the research and development effort of the industry is concentrated to meet the market demands within developed countries, while only a token effort is directed towards the Third World.

Table 11[63]

Transfer of technology to MNC subsidiaries in Brazil

	Number of subsidiaries
Basic research done in Brazil	Nil
Manufacture of some active ingredients in subsidiary	11
Formulation using imported raw materials	24

Table 12[26]

R & D facilities by US Pharmaceutical firms, 1965

	Personnel	*Expenditure ($ millions)*
US	16,530	304.1
Western Europe and Canada	1,675	24.5 (Western Europe and Canada and Underdeveloped Countries combined)
Underdeveloped Countries	410	

The technology of production of active pharmaceutical ingredients

The multinational firms establish production facilities in the underdeveloped countries, but often produce only comparatively old medicines using technology near the end or past its patent life. For the more modern medicines the Third World countries have to rely on the import of the active products without any possibility of technology transferring to them, or allowing a real chance for indigenous industry to learn the appropriate techniques. Thus in India, the majority of local production is started only about 10 years after the introduction of the product in the developed world. Of 138 drugs listed as major pharmaceutical innovations between 1950 and 1967, only 20 were being manufactured in India by 1972.[28]

The production of pharmaceuticals is usually covered by stringent patent protection. Local indigenous industry is prevented from using the processes or manufacturing the products that are covered by these patents taken out by the MNCs. This provides a monopoly situation, excluding local and foreign competition, and preventing price competition and local initiative. The majority of pharmaceutical patents in the developing countries are owned by the MNCs and are used not for production purposes in the Third World but for blocking purposes. In Colombia, out of 2,534 patents taken out by foreign firms in the pharmaceutical industry, less than ten were being used. Direct interviews with national firms indicated that, in the absence of patents, they could process about 90 per cent of the different products on the market, thus increasing their present production by about 300 per cent without significant changes in presently installed capacity.[6]

Table 13[28]

Production of pharmaceuticals in India (up to 1972)

Product	*Year of production in developed world*	*First year of production in India*
Dexamethasone	1959	Not produced
Pradnisone	1956	1963
Betamethasone	1960	not produced
Prednisolone	1956	1963
Triamcinolone	1959	not produced
Cortisone	1949	1957
Cortisol	1949	1957
Tetracyline	1952	1955
Teramycin	1950	1960
Aureomycin	1948	1955
Chloramphenicol	1948	1957
Kanamycin	1957	1969
Dihydrostrepto-mycin	1947	1963
Streptomycin	1947	1963
Cephalin	1961	not produced
Oxacillin	1963	not produced
Ampicillin	1961	not produced.
Phenoxymethyl penicillin	1953	1960
Penicillin G (large scale)	1945	1955
Frusemide	1966	not produced
Chlorpropamide	1958	1960
Tolbutamide	1955	1960
Acetazolamide	1956	1962
Sulphacetamide	1942	1953
Sulphathiazole	1939	1955
Sulphapyridine	1938	1955
Sulphanilamide	1935	1953

The finishing and formulation of pharmaceuticals

The technology involved in the production of tablets, capsules or fluids for injection etc. from the active ingredients is comparatively simple and often performed within the developing nations, either in subsidiaries of MNCs or as a joint venture with local industry. The amount of technology transferable at this stage is comparatively minor, but many hazards exist for those dealing with the MNCs.

National governmental pressure on the companies often leads to some form of joint venture or local formulation in the subsidiary whereby imported active ingredients are made into finished articles locally. The pricing of these intermediate materials will be dealt with in a later section of this book, but often the MNCs put other controls on these firms as a condition for their continuance in the venture. Obviously when the MNCs hold the supply of ingredients in this way, they are in a very strong bargaining position; infringement of the "rules" by national firms or governments might cause the cessation of supplies and a large loss of investment. The MNCs can make conditions for their subsidiaries and for the joint ventures from this very strong bargaining position. These conditions in the contracts, or tie-in clauses, have been studied in detail for the Colombian pharmaceutical industry.[12 10]

Import restrictions

A study of 51 contracts contained data in 35 regarding import practices. Of these, 33 explicitly required exclusive importation from the parent company of intermediate products. Follow-up of these products established an average of 155 per cent overpricing because of the elimination of competition through this tie-in clause.

Royalty payments

These are the payments made by the subsidiary to the parent-company for know-how. Because they are tax-deductible they are an attractive method of transferring returns to the parent company. Thus they were estimated to represent 14 per cent of the effective return to the parent as against declared profit of 3.4 per cent in the sample of the pharmaceutical industry studied. When these royalty payments were negotiated through the Colombian Government it resulted in a 104 per cent reduction in the value of royalties paid.

Export restrictions.

The use of these restrictions obviously decreases the value of the presence of foreign companies in the host country by making the subsidiary unable to earn foreign exchange. Of the firms studied, 85 per cent explicitly prohibited exports of manufactured goods from nationally owned firms and joint ventures, if such goods were produced using foreign technology.

By using this immense power over intermediate products, trading arrangements, patents and trademarks, the parent company is in a good position to limit the activities of its subsidiaries and those with whom it enters into joint ventures. Take-overs are frequent, with the bargaining so one-sided that "recent history is ripe with cases in which the contractor or licensee eventually became a wholly-owned subsidiary of the multinational firm".[26]

Thus rather than the benign transfer of technology that is often claimed, the picture is one in which the companies appear keen to use their power to *prevent* the transfer of technology and eliminate all but the most tenacious competition.

V

Some Economic Perspectives

There can be no doubt that the pharmaceutical industry is highly profitable for the multinational companies concerned, and that the companies make a substantial contribution to the balance of payments of the country which houses the parent company. There is debate, however, about the contribution that subsidiaries of the large firms make to the balance of payments when operating in other *developed* countries. The fullest estimate, taking into account imports, exports, royalty payments, the remission of profits and capital transfers, suggested that the presence in the UK of foreign-owned pharmaceutical companies has had virtually no effect on the UK balance of payments.[29] A substantial revision of this view would probably be necessary following the investigations of the Monopolies Commission into the activities of Roche Products in the UK, which found that they had made an excessive profit equal to approximately £25m over seven years in the sale of just two of their products. This represents a return in excess of 70 per cent per annum of capital employed (as defined by the Monopolies Commission). The Commission concluded, hardly surprisingly, that the pricing of Roche Products "operates and may be expected to operate against the public interest".[1]

It is not within the scope of this book to draw conclusions about the operations of the MNCs within the developed world, but we should certainly bear them in mind when attempting an analysis on the situation in the Third World.

As discussed in the previous sections, through control of technology the parent companies can exert a great amount of financial control over their subsidiaries, or partners, in the underdeveloped countries.

This control is exerted in three major ways:

i. Royalty remission, e.g. for the sale of technology or use of brand names.
ii. Tie-in clauses, preventing activities not controlled from the parent company.
iii. Sale of intermediate products or transfer pricing arrangements.

The first two means of financial control have been covered in the previous section, mainly detailing the empirical evidence available from Colombia. Evidence for the transfer pricing arrangements between parent and subsidiaries also comes mainly from Colombia, but there is no reason to suppose that the situation there is any different from elsewhere in the Third World, just that more data has been uncovered by diligent research.

Comparing the prices that firms were paying for intermediate products from the parent company with prices at which the same products could have been obtained in the world market, the Colombian investigators found overpricing in *every case.* This ranged up to the much quoted figure of 6,478 per cent for the active ingredient of diazepam and averaged out for all pharmaceutical products at 155 per cent.[10 and 12]

Table 14[10]

Product	*Multinational price of importation to Colombia (FOB) US $*	*Range of other quotations on world market (FOB) US $*	*Percentage over pricing*
Chlordiazepoxide	1,250.00	18.90 - 20.00	6,155
Diazepam	2,500.00	30.00 - 45.55	6,478
Ampicillin	420.00	162.50 - 200	136.5
Tetracyline base	250.00	23.5	948.0
Erythromycin	275.56	132.00	108.7
Oxytetracycline	147.00	31.75	387.5
Promethazine	140.00	19.70	654.3
Triamcinolone	24,000.00	6,600.00	233.3
Neomycin	53.00	37.7	40.6
Dihydrostreptromycin	29.00	27.50	5.4
Chloramphenicol	27.00	13.5	100.0
Dexamethasone	27.50	7.10	267.0
Methyldopa	80.00	18.48	333.0
Indomethacin	640.00	72.5	611.0
Hydrochlorothiazide	90.00	5.20	1,530.7
Guanethidine	920.00	190.80	382.0
Metronidazole	390.00	11.15	3,398.0
Penicillin G	0.03 MU	0.018 MU	66.7

The conclusion from the Colombian work was that the effective return on net worth for the sector of the pharmaceutical industry studied was 136.3 percent which shows a marked discrepancy from the 6.7 per cent return on investment declared as profits for tax purposes by the companies concerned!

Actual returns (100 per cent) = Reported Profits 3.4 per cent + Royalties 14 per cent + Overpricing 82.6 per cent.

The effect of these financial arrangements on the governments of the underdeveloped countries, especially those faced with limited, or diminishing foreign exchange resources, is often to bring about an actural *reduction* over time in the quantity of medicines that can be imported into the country.

Sri Lanka, faced with a chronic foreign exchange problem and a 40-50 per cent increase in drug prices, found that the 1970 allocation of foreign exchange could buy only half the drugs purchased by the 1965 allocation.[30 and 31]

Table 15[30 and 31]

Sri Lankan Government Annual allocation of foreign exchange for drug imports. In millions of rupees.

1965	33.0
1966	31.38
1967	24.08
1968	28.78
1969	27.70
1970	24.357

The government-sponsored investigation studied the quantities and prices of medicines imported into the private sector of Sri Lanka and found that although 11,671,817 rupees had been spent in foreign exchange on these drugs in 1969, over 8 million rupees could have been saved by importing the same drugs in bulk through the Civil Medical Stores purchasing on the open market.

The actual mechanism by which price levels of finished products are fixed, in the various countries in which the companies operate, is a closely guarded secret. Virtually no information on price levels or price fixing mechanisms is published by any large pharmaceutical company. However, it is fair to surmise that the pricing structure is such as to maximise returns on investment. Our hypothesis is that this is hardly ever in the best interests for the relief of suffering of the maximum number of inhabitants of the Third World countries with strictly limited resources.

Table 16[30 and 31]

Comparison of annual import prices of drugs in private sector (actual) with prices if imported by Civil Medical Stores (hypothetical) (Sri Lanka)

	Private sector imports (cif value) 1,000 Rs	*Civil medical Stores purchase (fob price), 1,000 Rs*
Analgesics and anti-rheumatics	4,886	595
Hypnotics	59	22
Anticonvulsants	63	21
Electrolytes	178	65
Antimicrobials	3,730	1,797
Antacids	324	162
Antispasmodics	130	24
Antiprotozeal drugs	323	145
Uterine stimulants etc.	41	10
Antihistamines	471	98
Antidiabetic drugs	750	103
Cardiac drugs	44	11
Antianginal drugs	86	14
Anticoagulants	10	4
Antihypertensics	299	79
Diuretics	148	71
Anaesthetics	132	47

In general, the MNCs operate to produce and market modern medicines, usually still covered by patent protection and sold by brand name. Because of these protections from competition and through

Table 17

Comparative costs of therapies available in Tanzania (Prices in Tanzanian shillings) Speight (32)

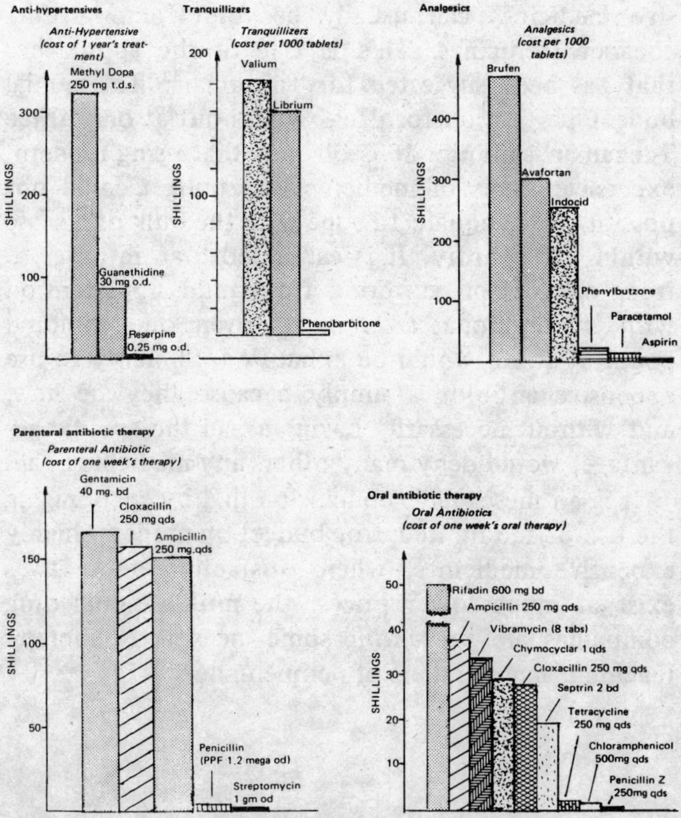

intensive advertising efforts, the price of these products are usually maintained at a high level. These modern drugs are much sought after within the Third World, because they are modern and are highly advertised, but they may in fact represent only a marginal improvement in therapeutic efficacy over older, cheaper, well tried preparations which are not covered by patents and are marketed under their generic names.

Thus an acceptable alternative to the new, expensive medicines can usually be found amongst the cheaper medicines. This is one of the approaches that has been suggested for Tanzania.[32] The annual budget per person for drugs works out at only three Tanzanian shillings. It is obvious that using modern, expensive types of medicines the budget could not possibly be adequate to cope with the bulk of disease within the country. It is estimated that, in order to treat one person suffering from mild hypertension with methyldopa *(Aldomet),* over one hundred peoples' quota would be exhausted. Similarly to use expensive antibiotics simply because they are new, and without necessarily having a real therapeutic advantage, would deny many others any medicine at all.

It is an inescapable conclusion that by encouraging the use of the limited drug budget on modern, highly expensive medicines, when satisfactory alternatives exist at much lower prices, the multinational drug companies are *preventing* some measure of therapy reaching large numbers of people in need.

VI

The Hard Sell

The promotional techniques for the sale of pharmaceutical products in the West are well know, and the cause of much heated argument, *but* they are at least subject to various statutory and voluntary controls. In the UK these include the Trade Descriptions Act (1968), the Medicines Act (1968) and a multitude of codes of practice for advertising issued by the Institute of British Advertisers, the Advertising Standards Authority, etc.

Although there are occasional advertisments and promotional activities that do not conform to these standards, and are obvious infringements of the law, or the spririt of voluntary controls, in general the debate is one of taste and emphasis rather than illegal practice and intentional deceit. More importantly we should consider if the sale of medicines should be promoted through intensive advertising at all, or should be subject to more rational appraisal of comparative efficacy and cost-benefit. This becomes even more important when applied to the competitive jungle of underdeveloped countries. In the absence of satisfactory statutory controls, and in a climate of often less critical consumer appreciation, the push from the drug companies to sell more of their products leads to practices that would be definite infringements of the standards prevalent in the West.

i. The pricing of medicines is of vital importance in the underdeveloped nations for the reasons outlined above. However, in the absence of statutory requirements insisting on the inclusion of absolute or comparative prices in the promotional literature, scant effort is made by the companies to comply with this "social requirement". Often no mention is made of the cost of medicines in advertisements, and the economic aspects of prescribing are rarely discussed in relation to supposed therapeutic advances introduced into the Third World.

ii. The effective therapeutic uses of any particular drug are largely internationally applicable. However, promotional literature often varies from country to country, depending on the market and national controls over promotional activity. Thus in the Third World some products are promoted for use in situations which can be of no therapeutic benefit and could possibly be very harmful. The most complete survey of this has been the collection of indications suggested by the manufacturers for the use of the antibiotic *chloramphenicol.*[33]

It is now generally accepted in the West that the systematic use of this drug should be restricted to the treatment of typhoid fever and haemophilus influenzae meningitis; with very occasional advantage it can be used as a second-choice antibiotic for other serious conditions. Responding to statutory controls, the manufacturers restrict its advocation to these few conditions in their literature in the UK but were found to be advertising the same medicine for a whole variety of inappropriate conditions in their literature aimed at the Third World:

Table 18[33]

Indications	*UK*	*Jamaica*	*Ceylon*	*Egypt*
Typhoid	+	+	+	+
H. influenzae meningitis	+	+		
Pertussis		+	+	+
Ricketsia		+	+	+
Bacterial meningitis			+	+
Brucellosis infections		+	+	
Genitourinary infections		+	+	+
Intestinal infections		+	+	+
Respiratory infections		+	+	+
Gynae infections			+	+
Veneral infections		+	+	+

Although the legal requirements were probably being met, the ethical implications are obvious.

iii. The survey also looked into the warnings that were included with the same antibiotic, *chloramphenicol.* There are eight main categories which may be considered absolute or relative contra-indications to the use of this drug. *None* was mentioned in the literature supplied by the manufacturers for the doctors' use in Egypt or Sri Lanka and only one contra-indication was mentioned in Jamaica.

Similarly there are definite side-effects that occasionally follow the use of this antibiotic, the most important of which is the potential aplastic anaemia (a fatal condition) that can, albeit rarely, follow its administration, especially in children. None of the literature studied for use in the Third World mentioned all the potential side effects.[34]

Table 19[33]

Warnings about major side effects	*UK*	*Jamaica*	*Ceylon*	*Egypt*
Allergy or hypersensitivity	+			
Blood bone-marrow effects	+++	++	++	
Gastro-intestinal effects	+			++

Although *chloramphenical* has received much attention, similar cases continue to be published regarding the promotion of other medicines within the Third World. Recently Winthrop advertised their product *Winstrol Compouna* (an anabolic steroid, *Stanozolol*) in a journal in Mexico. This compound was advocated for use in young children complaining of "poor appetite, fatigue or weight loss" and without any warning of adverse effects. Promotional literature in the USA restricts indications for the use of this drug to aplastic anaemia, osteoporoses and pituitary dwarfism, and is required by Federal Drugs Administration (FDA) law to include warnings about stunting of growth and testicular atrophy in boys and hirsuitism, male/pattern baldness; deepening of the voice and clitoral enlargement in females These are not rare idiosyncratic reactions, but will certainly occur if sufficient of the drug is administered. They are usually irreversible, even after prompt discontinuance of the drug . . . however the Winthrop advertisements did not mention any of these effects and gave no recommendations for limiting the duration of treatment.[36]

It is quite obvious that the safe and efficacious use of modern, powerful medicines relies on accurate information being given to the doctors who prescribe them. Where the quantity and type of information is not covered by statutory controls, the drug manufacturers seem unwilling to maintain the necessary standards on their own account. This is potentially dangerous to the inhabitants of the Third World, who will be left without adequate safeguards over the use of these medicines. It is therefore necessary to press for international control over the marketing techniques of the drug manufacturers to prevent further harm coming to the peoples of developing nations. The aim should be to ensure international uniformity of standards of drug information and to disseminate accurate information about pharmaceutical products regarding their therapeutic use and cost-benefit.[37]

VII

Department of Dirty Tricks

The testing of new medicines on the people of under-developed countries.

The testing of new products on human populations is governed by the Helsinki Declaration, which was published by the World Medical Association in 1964, and took over from the Nuremberg Code, developed at the end of World War II. Both these guidelines require voluntary, informed consent from the human subject, and the Federal Drugs Administration in the USA will not now grant a license to a new drug if the conditions of the Helsinki Declaration were not met during its testing. When medicines are tested in the Third World, it is obviously more difficult to be absolutely sure of the level of informed consent given by the subjects of experimentation.

The most flagrant use of the peoples of Third World countries for testing new products has been during the development of various contraceptive devices, and in particular the steroid contraceptives. The very first oral forms of these contraceptives were given their initial large-scale clinical trials around 1953 in Puerto Rico, Sponsored by G.D. Searle and Co.[39, 40] This was followed with various steroid preparations tested by the Ortho Research

Foundation and the Syntex Company in Puerto Rico, Haiti[41] and Mexico.[42] The first major clinical trial in the USA (also sponsored by Syntex and Ortho) at this time, used women from low-income groups of whom 84 per cent were of Mexican extraction and 6 per cent were Negroes.[43]

Further development of oral contraception depended heavily on research work done within the Third World, and sponsored directly by Western drug companies. The development of the first low-dose oral progesterones was researched in Chile, sponsored jointly by Syntex and Merck-Darmstadt (Germany). Even when using foreign women to experiment, the emphasis was on the illiterate of low-income groups, and these represented 345 of the 390 women tested in the trials.[44]

Other methods of contraception received their testing in this way, including various techniques for the use of intra-uterine devices,[45, 46] and more recently the addition of copper to these devices. This was initially tested in Chile[46] with large scale follow-up surveys in Colombia, Iran, Korea, Taiwan and Thailand.[46]

A product recently receiving much attention because of its potential as a widely distributable (and highly profitable) method of contraception, is the injectable steroid, *depo-medroxyprogesterone.* This is known as DMPA or *Depo-Provera,* and can be injected between twice and four times each year to achieve control of fertility. Although it is produced by the Upjohn Company of Kalamazoo, Michigan, it has so far not been approved for use either in the USA or in the UK. So far, though, it has been tested in Brazil, Thailand, Chile, Philippines, Sri Lanka,

Hong Kong, Egypt, Honduras, Peru, Mexico and Pakistan.[48 49 65]

When research into its possible effect on the weight and blood pressure of women taking the injections was carried out in South Africa, the researchers saw fit to examine these features by experimenting with Negro (75 per cent) and Asiatic (25 per cent) women, rather than on women with the same coloured skin as the researchers.[50]

The dumping of drugs

When medicine is banned from use in a developed country because of new evidence of toxicity, or lack of efficacy, it becomes an expensive prospect for the company that has produced it. Because of the international variability of control procedures, it is usually possible for the companies to continue to sell the banned product abroad.

This is not restricted to dumping of banned products in the Third World, and is well illustrated by export from the USA of a great number of medicines and food additives, not allowed by the FDA for use within the USA. Thus many medicines and food additives are produced in the USA, or by subsidiaries of US firms, that would not pass the laws for home consumption. Although there is now a long list of these products, perhaps the best example is the use of cyclamates in goods for export. The best illustrated case documenting the dumping of medicines in the Third World is the selling of over 10 million capsules of *chloramphenical* by Parke-Davis, through the US Defence Department to the clinics of South Vietnam,[34] shortly after it had been banned for use the USA.

Illegal acts by the drug companies

Although the first paragraphs of this chapter describe activities that are hardly desirable when considered from the viewpoint of the inhabitants of the Third World, they are usually still within the law. There do remain commercial activities for which this probably cannot be said.

A. ILLEGAL TRAFFIC

The importing and exporting of all products is of course subject to control and taxation by the governments of the countries involved. In Chile under the Allende government, Pfizer's subsidiary was accused of smuggling drugs illegally across the border to Bolivia and Peru. The Government felt that the only way to prevent such activities was state control of the company. Unfortunately the military coup of September 1973 prevented the legal case reaching any conclusion. Another incident which exhibits the scope of these companies for illegal trafficking is the case of the subsidiary of a European MNC which was importing less than 30 per cent of declared contents in sealed packing cases imported into a South American country.[52] By paying 100 per cent of reported cost to the parent company (through a tax-refuge) it was able to transfer 300 per cent increased profits to the parent.

B. ILLEGAL SALES TECHNIQUES

Although this is one of the most difficult areas of all to actually prove, rumours abound. During the intense pressure-selling of many medicines it is certain that favours and bribes, even new cars, change hands. Perhaps the nearest case to prove this point is the two government pharmaceutical buyers now in prison in Kenya for accepting bribes from *Roche* products for favouring their products when spending the Government's medicine budget.

The response of the Third World.

Our analysis so far leads us to conclude that a proportion of the multinational pharmaceutical industry has small regard for social ends. Their insistence on manufacturing and marketing highly sophisticated, expensive products for routine use within developed countries cannot be to the advantage of the majority of the population unable to afford them. The present structuring of the industry prevents the teaching of relevant technological skills at a satisfactory rate, and the functioning of the subsidiaries within the Third World is a very sizeable drain of scarce financial resources. Where poor controls exist over the functions of the industry, it has shown itself unable to control itself and impose restraints that would prevent exploitation in the countries where it operates.

How have the Third World countries themselves perceived this industry, and if their analysis is similar to ours, what have they attempted to do about it? Have any of their attempts to break out of this pattern been resisted by the multinational companies trying to protect their continuing interest in maintaining the *status quo?*

In each country there will be a struggle between the supporters of the multinational companies who see the way to development through increasing cooperation with the present holders of technological power, and those who believe that radical change is necessary to break away from this unhealthy influence and establish independent lines of development. Our analysis would seem to support the latter view, and we shall now examine that progress has been made towards the goal of technological independence in various Third World countries.

Moves towards legislation on the influx of technology
Several official international organisations have recommended the establishment of both national and international bodies to examine technology transfers and to explore alternative means of acquiring technology for the less developed countres. The most important recommendations along these lines come from the United Nations Committee on Trade and Development (UNCTAD)[66] and from the UN Department of Economic and Social Affairs.[53]

Various piecemeal attempts at legislation along the lines of the recommendations and proposals from these august bodies have followed, both generally, and specifically, for the pharmaceutical industry. Thus the Indian Government set up a five-member committee to scrutinise technology reports,[45] and one part of the recommendations for the Sri Lanka pharmaceutical industry was to modify the patent laws and abolish the mechanism for patenting pharmaceutical products. It has already been mentioned that the Colombian Government insisted on negotiation of royalty payments through government channels and that this resulted in over 100 per cent saving on these payments.

However, the most comprehensive attempt so far at legislation has come from the Mexican Government.[55] They have passed an Act which attempts, not to curb or hamper the import of foreign technology, but to fit the technology to the needs of the country. As well as providing for financial surveillance over all deals, it is an attempt to make sure that much-needed technology is available to the country, and that inappropriate technology is excluded. It is neither revolutionary nor confiscatory legislation, but a concerted attempt to redress the balance of bargaining power between the MNCs and the governments of the Third World. The Act came into force only very recently and its implementation and enforcement will be studied with great interest.

The switch to generic names

A large part of the power of the pharmaceutical companies lies in their use of brand names. Thus, although exactly the same product might be available at a fraction of the cost under its generic name, the doctors and general public are used to prescriptions of brand-name products. The major fear is that if generic names only are used the quality of medicines will decline. It is thought that a considerable protection is afforded by the use of brand names because the companies concerned will be keen to maintain the quality of their product, as it is easily identified by brand name. Obviously any moves to abolish the use of brand names, without adequate quality control over the generic product, will be doomed to such accusations and presents a very real possibility of the introduction of poor quality products.

The first country to insist on marketing of drugs by generic name was Pakistan.[56] Following the implementation of the Drug (Generic Names) Act in March 1973, a tremendous uproar has ensued with accusations of flooding of the markets with poor quality products and a proliferation of back-street production by "ghost" manufacturers. It is hard to evaluate the exact truth of these rumours and it certainly would be in the interests of the foreign manufacturers to fan the fires of these stories and press for the re-introduction of brand names. The pressure from these MNCs has been considerable: Ciba-Geigy pulled out of all operations in Pakistan as a protest against the use of generic names, and pressure from other firms led to extended permission of the use of 244 brand-named products for 18 months after the implementation of the Act.[57]

In India the Hathi Committee has recommended the "debranding" of 16 essential drugs for a trial period. Very conscious of the confused situation in Pakistan, they also made a series of suggestions for measures to improve quality control standards. Already the pharmaceutical industry has made a declaration against the proposals of the Committee.[58]

The proposals for the management of pharmaceuticals in Sri Lanka have included the use of generic names rather than brand names in their comprehensive plans for the future; many other countries have plans which include restriction of pharmaceuticals to those approved by government in National Formularies using exclusively generic names.

The establishment of national puchasing and distribution

The purchasing in the open market of the cheapest effective drugs available, coupled with quality control and distribution under government supervision would serve as a very effective interim way of rationalising the supply of drugs to the population of a Third World country, before a sufficient indigenous pharmaceutical industry could be established. This is the approach that has found favour with the Sri Lankan Government. The two-thirds savings that are possible have already been detailed in Table 16, and this scheme should be the model for those attempting an approach of this nature. Quality control is ensured by routine government surveillance, and a distinguished Formulary Committee meets regularly to consider new applications for inclusion on the approved National Formulary. In this way innovations are rapidly included, and obsolete or dangerous drugs can be eliminated. Drug information is rapidly disseminated through the regular publication of Formulary Notes and the education of medical practitioners continues in the most efficient and cost-effective manner. The importation of over 3,000 pharmaceutical preparations has been reduced to 800; advertising and the use of brand names have been abolished.[30, 31]

Attempts have been made by other governments to ensure more control over drug prices and distribution. The Indian Government has a Drugs (Price Control) Order which has a formula for the amount of profit that can be made on 18 basic drugs and their 69 formulations. However, a piecemeal approach is not really likely to succeed and the failure of the drug firms to release sufficient information about their financial structure leads to real difficulties in implementation.[59]

In Egypt there is some centralisation of control and the total number of products distributed has been reduced from about 20,000 to 3,700. There is an official National Formulary containing about

2,500 drugs but lack of regular revision diminishes its use. Distribution of the drugs is made through a special company and product control is centralised, leading to virtual equality in the supply of effective products to even remote rural areas.[60]

The establishment of an independent pharmaceutical industry within the developing nations

The establishment of viable indigenous industry must be the long-term solution that we advocate for the countries of the Third World.

There is evidence that this is presently within the technological capacity of the more advanced Third World nations and that if the barriers to the control of knowledge were lifted, the developing nations would be able, almost immediately, to become self-sufficient in the basic formulations. Interviews in Colombia sugggested that the national industry had the technical knowledge and production capacity already installed to manufacture about 90 per cent of currently available drugs. The experience gained would soon lead to complete replacement of dependence on foreign imports.

The nationalised Indian industry undertakes independent research and development of new products. By consistent investment and concentration on one therapeutic field, Hindustan Antibiotics has recently developed and marketed two new antifungal antibiotics, which have been licensed for production in the USA.[28]

Many countries have State-sponsored plans to develop an indigenous pharmaceutical industry, but possibly the most encouraging start has been made in Egypt. The nationalised industry there has been able to purchase licenses to produce pharmaceuticals at a reasonable cost.

Now although production costs are relatively high, the industry produces 87 per cent of the needs of the Egyptian market and prices of the medicines are lower than the import prices of the same products.[61] The industry provides employment for over 17,000 workers and contributes about LE 8 million to offset the balance of payments. Between 1960 and 1965 consumption of drugs in Egypt increased by 128 per cent while total expenditure on foreign currency (including purchase of technology and necessary raw materials) increased by a mere 44 per cent.[61]

. . . that no man shall want

> "It is our business to see that no man shall want for what medicines might readily do."
>
> *Maurice King*[62]

It has not been our intention to attack the multinational pharmaceutical industry indiscriminately. Our task has been to study whether the present structure of the industry is capable of supplying the unmet needs within the Third World. The inhabitants of the entire world have a similar right to a full range of appropriate therapeutic products and the system by which these are supplied is an area of legitimate concern.

The development of the multinational pharmaceutical industry has led to the evolution of the present structure whereby the emphasis is placed on new products, protected by various controls and aggressively marketed. These new medicines are usually expensive and by definition must be highly profitable to pay back promotional and development costs.

The rationale behind this system is under examination in the developed world, and it certainly appears that it is incapable of meeting the real needs of the people of the Third World at present. The system is secretive and protective, preventing the spread of the portions of relevant technology that would make the developing world independent of the multinational companies. It is selective, concentrating its efforts on developing and marketing products that can only be of marginal use in conquering the majority of diseases in the developing nations. It is expensive to the countries within which it operates, draining them of foreign reserves, possibly serving to exacerbate the problems of national poverty that are the cause of most disease. Finally it is expensive in human terms, denying the majority of the people of the Third World countries the appropriate range of medicine that it is surely now technically feasible to supply.

There is increasing awareness that the methods, structure and functioning of all multinational companies in the developed and developing world needs very careful monitoring. This awareness is reflected in the recent wealth of literature on the subject[68, 3] and in the reports of a great many official organisations.[4, 26, 53, 55, 67]

The particular problems of control over the multinational pharmaceutical industry in some ways illustrate the general problems, and also pose a series of problems particular to the nature of the industry and the importance of the product.

The following series of recommendations is therefore a summary of the proposals made in three of the most recent United Nations documents concerning themselves with control over the multinational companies and the particular problems of the transfer of pharmaceutical technology to the developing nations.[53 66 67]

1. *Increasing the control over the multinational companies as presently organised.*
   i. An international information and research centre should be established under the aegis of the United Nations to document the activities of the multinational companies.
   ii. An enforceable code of conduct should be established to govern the activities of multinational companies.
   iii International standards of disclosure, accounting and reporting should be introduced, including data of relevance for the purpose of collective bargaining by the companies' labour force.
   iv. There should be revision of international laws regarding taxation which would include control over the intra-company transfer of assets.
   v. International agreed labour standards should be introduced, including standards of health and safety at work, free collective bargaining and equal treatment of workers.
   vi. International patenting procedures should undergo critical review.
   vii. There should be international standardisation of codes of advertising practice.

viii. Specialised training programme should be developed to teach personnel the specialised techniques required to negotiate with multinational concerns.

ix. Priority should be given to the establishment of groups of developing nations with joint policies as a means of improving their bargaining position. This would include improving control over choice, cost and conditions of acquiring technology from multinational companies.

2. Action at national level to improve purchasing and distribution of medicines

i. A National Formulary Committee should be established to draw up a list of approved, essential medicines.

ii. There should be a change to use of generic names only for these medicines.

iii. Purchasing procedures for these medicines should be centralised so that they can be bought at the cheapest available price on the world market.

iv. Measures should be taken to ensure that quality control procedures are developed to ensure the quality of medicines purchased.

v. Distribution of medicines should be improved.

vi. Regular information should be disseminated to medical practitioners about the medicines supplied. This should include information regarding the new additions to the National Formulary and details regarding pharmacological properties of approved medicines.

3. Establishment of indigenous pharmaceutical industry in developing nations

i. Establishment of an independent pharmaceutical industry should be encouraged within developing nations where possible. This will only be possible where there is also a well-developed production capability of basic chemical products.

ii. Where this capability does not exist the multinational companies should be required to establish basic drug producing facilities at a much faster rate.

iii. Where appropriate older technology can be acquired at a low cost for production of medicines of equal efficacy to the products of the multinational companies, this should be contemplated by developing nations.

iv. Where none of these measures would appear to be possible in the near future, cooperative development of the drug industry should be contemplated through the establishment of Cooperative Pharmaceutical Production and Technology Centres (COPPTECs).

The following objectives have been suggested:

a. to conduct research and development into the specific medicinal needs of developing countries not satisfactorily investigated by the existing research and development activities in developed countries;

b. to conduct R & D into improving and adapting technology copied or bought from the developed countries;

c. to collect technological, chemical and medical information relevant to the production, distribution and use of drugs;

d. collect financial and price data relevant to the negotiations of purchases of chemicals, technology and other services from the developed countries;

e. to collaborate and exchange information with drug authorities, medical research centres and other institutions in developed countries;

f. to engage in the production of basic chemicals needed for the setting up of drug formulation facilities in the participating countries.

Appendix[70]

General Pattern of "First-Line" Pharmaceuticals for a Developing Country

The following list is intended to portray the "typical" pattern of "first-line" drugs for a developing country. It is meant to contain the basic pharmaceuticals needed by small and medium-sized rural health units performing primary care in one of the least developed countries. On the (idealised) assumption that there is a mass rural health service, most health care contacts will be taking place at this level and these will be the drugs needed in the greatest quantities.

It must be emphasised that this list is intended to portray a *general pattern* of such pharmaceuticals for illustrative purposes, and it is neither precise nor exhaustive. No list can be prepared accurately without a study of the prevalent disease pattern and of the nature of the patient-contacts with the health service in a particular country.

The pharmaceuticals are listed mainly by therapeutic categories, rather than by specific names. This is because one of the important variables which determines whether or not a drug can be included in the first-line category is its cost. In this paper, pharmaceutical cost is not something that is being prejudged, since there may be cheaper alternatives for drugs (obtained either by local production or by importation) than, for example, the expensive products marketed by the multinational corporations. However, for the purposes of illustration only, some of the currently cheaper products, which could be included in this list without changing the usual sources of importation, are sometimes named as examples.

Vaccines

BCG (against tuberculosis)
  Smallpox (?)
Triple (whooping-cough, diphtheria, tetanus toxoid)
Poliomyelitis
Measles
Tetanus toxoid

Antibiotics for general internal use

Possibly three or four different types; for oral use, and one or two also by injection (e.g. penicillin-V oral, penicillin-G injection, a longer-acting penicillin injection; tetracycline; a sulphonamide; sterile diluent water for injection)

Antibiotics for external use

One or two each for skin, eyes and ears.

Other skin preparations

Anti-fungal applications (e.g., Whitfield's ointment)
Anti-scabies application (e.g., benzyl benzoate)
Anti-lice application (e.g., DDT)
Antiseptics (for general use; for obstetric use; for newborn babies)
Calamine applications and basic emulsifying ointments for "muscle" pains.

Anti-parasite preparations

Anti-malaria (e.g., chloroquine, mostly oral, also injection; possibly one other anti-malarial drug)

Anti-roundworm and anti-threadworm (e.g., piperazine)

Anti-hookworm (e.g., tetrachlorethylene or an alternative)

Possibly two-four other anti-parasite drugs depending on disease prevalence (e.g., amoebiasis, giardiasis, bilharzia)

Nutritional preparations

Vitamins (two or three preparations)

Iron (one or two preparations)

Anti-infective drugs for specific communicable disease control

Some of these agents may already have been included in the categories above. The number and nature of them may be determined by specially organised national programmes against these diseases. Examples are: anti-tuberculosis drugs (two or three), anti-leprosy drugs (one or two)

For diarrhoea

For re-hydration by oral route: bulk salt, potassium chloride and glucose or sugar.

For re-hydration by venous route: one or two infusion fluids

Anti-peristaltic preparation

For general use

Aspirin

One stronger pain-killer

Cough mixture

Anti-wheezing drug
"Dyspepsia" mixture
Anti-vomiting drug (by injection)
Preparation for constipation
Anti-convulsants (one or two, oral and injection)
One or two heart preparations (?)
One tranquiliser (?)

For obstetrics and gynaecology

Ergometrine injection
Pain-killer
Vaginal pessaries (one or two)
Special preparations for newborn (two or three)

For accidents

Gauze
Bandages
Splints
Catgut or thread

For laboratory

Basic chemicals, stains, etc.

Total separate active ingredients*: 50-60 (excluding laboratory reagents)

* Some active ingredients may appear in more than one formulation.

References

1. The Monopolies Commission (1973): Cholordiazepoxide and Diazepam, HMSO, 1973.
2. Müller, R., "The Multinational Companies and the Underdevelopment of the Third World," Ch. in *The Political Economy of Development and Underdevelopment,* ed. Charles Wilmer, New York, Random House, 1974.
3. Somavia.J., "Transnational Corporations: Information gathering by the United Nations," *Development Dialogue,* 1974, No. 2, p.11.
4. "Multinational Enterprises and Social Policy," ILO, Geneva, 1973, *Studies and Reports,* No.79.
5. Penrose, E.T., "International Patenting and the Less Developed Countries," *Economic Journal,* September 1973, p.768.
6. Vaitsos, C.V., "Patents Revisited: Their function in developing countries," *"Journal of Development Studies,* Vol. 9 No. 1, October 1972.
7. "Socio-economic progress in Latin America," Inter-American Development Bank (IDB), Washington DC, 1971.
8. Diaz, P., (1971) Andean Group Document, Quoted in Müller, op.cit.
9. Taft Morris, C., and Adleman, I., "An anatomy of income distribution patterns in developing nations," IDBR Economic Staff Paper, Washington, No. 116, September 1971.
10. Vaitsos, C.V., *Intercountry Income Distribution and Transnational Enterprises,* Oxford Clarendon, 1974.
11. Lall, S., (1973) "Transfer Pricing by Multinational Manufacturing Firms," *Oxford Bulletin of Economics and Statistics,* Vol. 35, No.3, p.173.

12. Vaitsos, C.V., "Transfer of resources and reservations of monopoly rents," *Economic Development Report,* No. 168, Harvard Advisory Service, Harvard, 1970.
13. Fajnzylber, F., CEPAL, November 1971. Quoted in Müller, op. cit.
14. Schifrin, G., "Thalidomide and beyond: Some recommendations regarding public policies towards the ethical drug industry," *Int. Journal of Health Services,* Vol. 4, No. 1 , 1974, p.147.
15. Powers, J., "Multinational Corporations in the light of the United Nations Report," Speech to the IFPMA: Mexico City November 1974, mimeo.
16. Powles, J., (1973) "On the limitations of modern medicine," *Science, Medicine and Man,* Vol.i, pp.1-30.
17. National Economic Development Office, 1972: "Focus on Pharmaceuticals," HMSO.
18. The Monopolies Commission, 1972: "Beecham-Glaxo. Boots. A report on the proposed merger," HMSO, Appendix 5.
19. Spinks, A., Quoted in Weatherall M., "Limitations on the supply and discovery of medicines," *Proc. Roy. Soc. Med,* Vol.67, December 1974.
20. Pharmaceutical Manufacturers' Association, *Factbook,* 1973. Washington.
21. Silverman, M., and Lee, P.R., *Pills, Profits and Politics,* University of California, Berkeley, 1974.
22. Dunlop, D., *Medicines in our time,* Nuffield Provincial Hospitals' Trust, London, 1973.
23. In addition to the official reports 1, 17 and 18 and op. cits. 21 and 22, a perspective on the industry can be obtained from reading:
    a. Teeling-Smith, *Innovation and the balance of payments,* Office of Health Economics, London, 1970.
    b. Cooper, H.M., *Prices and Profits in the Pharmaceutical Industry,* Pergamon Press, Oxford, 1966.
    c. Davies, W., *The Pharmaceutical Industry,* Pergamon Press, Oxford, 1967.
    d. Levinson, C., *The Multinational Pharmaceutical Industry,* International Federation of Chemical and General Workers, Geneva, 1974.
    e. Robson, J., "Take a Pill. The Drug Industry, private or Public?" *Marxists in Medicine,* London, 1972.
24. Weatherall, M., 1974, op. cit.

25. United National International Yearbook of Trade Statistics, 1972-3.
26. Wortzel, L.H., "Technology transfer in the Pharmaceutical Industry," UNITAR Research Report No. 14, Washington, 1971.
27. Lall, S., "The International Pharmaceutical Industry and Less-developed countries," *Oxford Bulletin of Economics and Statistics,* August 1974, p.143.
28. Ramachandra, P.K., and Ranrao, B.V., "The Pharmaceutical Industry in India," *Economic and Political Weekly,* Vol. VII. No. 9, 1972.
29. Lee, M., & Jones, R.H., (1970) "International Balance of Payments in the Pharmaceutical Industry," In *The International Pattern of Finance,* Ed. Teeling-Smith, op. cit.
30. Wickremasinghe, S.A., & Bibile, S., *The Management of Pharmaceuticals in Ceylon,* Report to the Hon, The Prime Minister, Industrial Development Board, Colombo, October 1970.
31. Wickremasinghe & Bibile, *British Medical Journal,* September 1971, 3, p.757.
32. Speight, N.N.P., "Cost-effectiveness and drug therapy," *Tropical Doctor,* April 1975, p.89.
33. Dunne, M., et. al., "Indications and warnings about Chloramphenenicol," *Lancet,* October 6 1973, pp.781-783.
34. Sesser, S., "Peddling dangerous drugs abroad," *New Republic,* March 6 1971, p.161.
35. Schrier, H.A., & Berger, L., "On Medical Imperialism." *Lancet,* June 8 1974, p.1161.
36. "Promotion of Drugs in Latin America," *Med. Lett. Drugs Ther.,* 1973, Vol 15, p.28.
37. Herxheimer, A., "Drug Information. Is there a need for international uniformity?" *Drugs* 8: 321-329, 1974.
38. Editorial, *The Journal of Laboratory and Clinical Medicine,* March 1974, Vol. 83, No. 3, p.339.
39. Garcia, C.R., et. al., *American Journal of Obstetric Gynaecology,* 1958, 75, 82.
40. Rice-Wray, E. "Field Study with Enovid as contraceptive agent," *Proceedings, symposium on 19-nor progestational steroids,* Chicago, G. D. Searle and Co., 1957.
41. Garcia, C.R., et. al., "Effectiveness of oral contraception," *Science,* 130: 81, 1959.
42. Rice-Wray, E., "Long-term administration of Norethin-

drone in fertility control," *JAMA*, Vol. 180, No. 5, 1962, p.355.
43. Goldzieher, J.W., "Study of Norethindrone in contraception," *JAMA*, Vol. 180, No. 5, 1962, p.359.
44. Zanartu, J., "Antifertility effect on continous low-dosage oral progesterone therapy," *BMJ*, 1968, 2, pp. 263-266.
45. Godsmith, A., *American Journal of Obstetric Gynae.*, 112, 957, 1972.
46. Hue, K., *American Journal of Obstetric Gynae.*, April 1974, p.975.
47. Tatum, H.J., *American Journal of Obstetric Gynae.*, Vol. 117, No. 5, p.602, 1973.
48. Vecchio, T.J. "Depo-Provera contraception. International experience in over 20,000 cases," *J Reproductive Medicine*, Vol.8, 1972, p.208.
49. McDaniel, E.B. *American Journal of Obstetric Gynae*, Vol. 119, No. 2, 1974, p.175.
50. Leiman, G., *American Journal of Obstetric Gynae*, Vol. 114, No. 1 1972, p.97.
51. Levinson, C., *The Multinational Pharmaceutical Industry*, op. cit.
52. Müller, R., op. cit.
53. *The Impact of Multinational Corporations on Development and on International Relations*, United Nations Group of 20 Eminent Persons' Report, E-74.11.X. 5-.
54. SCRIP. 12.9.74.
55. Wionczek, M.S., "The first developing country to legislate the influx of technology," *Ceres*, March 1973.
56. Herxheimer, A., "Using Generic Names. Pakistan Leads the World," *Drug Ther. Bull*, 10.60, July 1972.
57. SCRIP, 7.6.74.
58. SCRIP, 5.10.74 and 24.10.74.
59. Mote, V. L., & Pathak, H. N. "Drug price control; an evaluation," *Economic and Political Weekly*, July 1972, p.1369.
60. Friebel, H. (1973) *WHO exploratory mission on drug production, distribution control and utilisation in Egypt*, WHO EMRO/73/1917.
61. Handoussa, H., *A case study of Egypt's Pharmaceutical Industry*, Unpublished PhD, London University, August 1974.
62. King, M., "Medicine in Red and Blue," *Lancet* i p.679, 1972.

63. Bertero. C.O., *Drugs and dependancy in Brazil. An empirical study of dependency theory. The case of the pharmaceutical industry,* PhD thesis, Cornell University, August 1972.
64. *The Pharmaceutical Industries in the Second Development Decade,* UNIDO Secretariat, May 1969, p.19.
65. *Population Report,* Series K, March 1975, George Washington University Medical Centre, Washington DC.
66. Lall, S., *Major issues in transfer of technology in developing countries.* A case study of the pharmaceutical industry, *UNCTAD/TD/B/C. 6/4, October 1975.*
67. Restrictive business practices. Review of major developments in the area of restrictive business practices, UNCTAD Secretariat, TD/8/C.2/159, April 1975.
68. Barnet, R., and Müller, R., *Global Reach,* New York, Simon & Schuster, 1975.
69. Frank, A.G., "The Development of Underdevelopment," *Monthly Review,* Vol 18, No. 4, 1966.
70. Segall, M., *Pharmaceuticals and Health Planning in developing countries.* I.D.S. Communication 119, University of Sussex 1976. This Appendix is reproduced by permission of Malcolm Segall.
71. Abel-Smith, *An International Study of health expenditure,* WHO Public Health paper 32, 1967, p.64.